First Library of Knowledge

Cultures of the Past

BLACKBIRCH PRESS

An imprint of Thomson Gale, a part of The Thomson Corporation

Detroit • New York • San Francisco • San Diego • New Haven, Conn. • Waterville, Maine • London • Munich

THOMSON

GALE

First published in 2006 by Orpheus Books Ltd., 6 Church Green, Witney, Oxfordshire, OX28 4AW

First published in North America in 2006 by Thomson Gale

Copyright © 2005 Orpheus Books Ltd.

Created and produced: Rachel Coombs, Nicholas Harris, Sarah Hartley, Orpheus Books Ltd.

Text: Julia Bruce

Consultant: Philip Wilkinson

Illustrators: Peter Dennis, Steve Noon, Nicky Palin, and Mark Stacey

For more information, contact
Blackbirch Press
27500 Drake Rd.
Farmington Hills, MI 48331-3535
Or you can visit our Internet site at http://www.gale.com

LIBRARY OF CONGRESS CATALOGING-IN-PUBLICATIONS

Bruce, Julia.
  Cultures of the past / by Julia Bruce.
    p. cm. -- (First library of knowledge)
  Originally published: Oxfordshire, UK : Orpheus Books, 2006.
  Includes bibliographical references.
  ISBN 1-4103-0344-6 (hardcover : alk. paper) 1. History of cultures-- Juvenile literature. I. Title. II. Series.

Printed in Malaysia
10 9 8 7 6 5 4 3 2 1

CONTENTS

3 INTRODUCTION

4 THE VIKINGS

6 THE CRUSADES

8 A MEDIEVAL CASTLE

10 A CITY IN THE MIDDLE AGES

12 CHINA IN THE MIDDLE AGES

14 THE SAMURAI

16 AMERICA BEFORE COLUMBUS

18 PIRATES

20 CAPTAIN COOK

22 THE PLAINS INDIANS

24 THE GOLD RUSH

26 A WILD WEST TOWN

28 A ZULU VILLAGE

30 A STREET 150 YEARS AGO

32 GLOSSARY

32 INDEX

INTRODUCTION

IMAGINE you could travel back to 1,000 years ago. You might visit the seafaring Vikings, or march alongside crusading knights in Jerusalem. Hundreds of years later, you could drop in on the Inca Empire, sail the South Seas with Captain James Cook, or explore the Wild West. What was it like to live in these exciting places so many years ago?

THE VIKINGS

THE VIKINGS lived around a thousand years ago in Norway, Sweden, and Denmark. They were skilled sailors and craftspeople. In their famous longboats, they explored as far as North America. They were also warlike and often raided coastal towns and villages.

LIFE IN A VIKING TOWN

The harbor was the most important place in a Viking town. Here, boats were loaded and unloaded with goods and animals. Markets were set up on the dock. Nearby, boat-builders, potters, leatherworkers, carpenters, and other craftspeople were busy in their workshops. Their cottages had walls made of wood and thatched roofs.

longship

dock

harbor

thatching

baker's oven

warriors

well

leather-working

hanging hides

splitting wood

blacksmith

weaving

assembly hall

market

THE CRUSADES

THE CRUSADES were wars between Christians and Muslims. They began when the great Christian city of Constantinople was threatened by a Muslim invasion in the 11th century.

CRUSADERS

From all over Europe, knights and ordinary men volunteered to be crusaders. They formed armies and set off for Constantinople. They fought many battles and, in 1099, captured the holy city of Jerusalem from Muslim forces. The crusaders held onto it for nearly 100 years.

CASTLES AND FIGHTING MONKS

The Knights Templar and the St. John's Hospitallers were crusaders dedicated to defending Jerusalem. They were known as fighting monks and built great castles (below) to protect the land they had gained around Jerusalem. The Hospitallers also tended the wounded.

Saladin was a deeply religious and honorable man. He was also a great military leader and won many battles against the crusaders.

SALADIN AND SARACENS

Saladin, the sultan of Egypt, united many small Muslim states in the Middle East and raised a great army. The crusaders called these Muslims Saracens. They were fine horsemen and brave fighters. In 1187 Saladin's army recaptured Jerusalem. Saladin organized a peace treaty, but other Crusades followed. Land in the area changed hands more times. The Crusades finally ended around 1300.

A Medieval Castle

CASTLES were built by kings and lords to defend their lands. They had thick, high walls topped with battlements, and were often surrounded by a moat. The main building was called a keep.

keep

solar (lord's private apartment)

great hall

chapel

stores

stores

kitchens

bailey

well

blacksmith's forge

stables

LIFE IN A CASTLE

The keep was where the lord and his family lived. They dined in the great hall. The lord's servants worked in the forge, kitchens, and stores as well as the stables in the bailey—the castle courtyard.

A knight served a king or lord as a soldier. He underwent many years of training to learn fighting skills. Knights were expected to follow a code of good behavior. They took part in tournaments that featured jousting contests.

battlements

jousting tournament

moat

stores

portcullis

gatehouse

drawbridge

walls

dungeons

A CITY IN THE MIDDLE AGES

LIFE was busy in a medieval city. Lots of people lived and worked here. Strong stone walls protected the city and guards controlled who came through its gates. Inside, buildings were crammed together along narrow, winding streets.

fish market

merchant's house

LIFE IN THE CITY

A medieval city was a very dirty, smelly, and noisy place. The crowded streets were full of shops. The busy markets sold food grown in farms outside the city. Merchants brought silks, spices, and precious metals from abroad. City craftspeople, such as potters and blacksmiths, made goods to trade with the merchants. People came from miles around to pray in the cathedral. Its huge size showed everyone how rich the city was.

CHINA IN THE MIDDLE AGES

CHINA was the richest country in the world in the Middle Ages. But it was always threatened by tribes to the north. In the 1200s, the Mongols conquered China.

Kublai Khan loved hunting and was a great horseman. He often hunted with a leopard that rode with him on the back of his horse.

CHINA'S CAPITALS

Chang'an was China's first capital city. It stood at the beginning of the Silk Road, a trading route between East and West, in central China. It had great palaces, fabulous pagodas, and beautiful gardens. The new Mongol emperor, Kublai Khan, made Cambaluc (Beijing) in the far north his capital city.

Most people in medieval China were farmers. The crops they grew fed not only themselves but also the army and people in the cities.

Kublai Khan was the first foreign emperor of China. He was a very wise and tolerant ruler.

MARCO POLO

Kublai Khan encouraged foreign visitors to his magnificent court. Marco Polo came from Venice in 1275. He was the emperor's loyal servant for eighteen years and traveled around the Chinese Empire.

Marco Polo and his father and uncle bow low before Kublai Khan. Polo wrote a best-selling book about his amazing travels.

SUMMER PALACE

Kublai Khan's summer palace at Shangdu was the most splendid. It had marble and gold walls. Its golden ceilings were studded with rubies and diamonds.

CHINESE JUNKS

Marco Polo sailed around the coast of Asia in a sturdy Chinese boat called a junk. Junks had sails supported by bamboo masts. The largest junk could carry 600 people. During the 15th century, the Chinese explorer Zheng He sailed to India, Arabia, and Africa in a large junk.

THE SAMURAI

THE SAMURAI were brave Japanese warriors. They became very powerful in medieval times when Japan was torn apart by wars between enemy clans.

Finally, a samurai leader took power and became the shogun, a military dictator. The shoguns ruled Japan on behalf of the emperor for the next 700 years.

SAMURAI CASTLES

The first samurai were farmers. When they were not fighting, they went home to tend their farms. They became skilled in martial arts and were expert horsemen. The mightiest samurai held high positions at court and lived in fine castles to show off their power. The *tenshu*, the main building of the samurai castle, was several stories high. It was protected by thick walls and sometimes had a moat.

Samurai armor was made of metal or leather plates laced together. All samurai carried a pair of curved swords (*daisho*) and often wore masks molded into terrifying faces.

AMERICA BEFORE COLUMBUS

MANY DIFFERENT peoples lived in the Americas before they were discovered by Europeans. The Aztec, Inca, and Maya built great civilizations. These were all destroyed by the Spanish conquistadors (conquerors) in the 16th century.

THE INCA

The Inca were a wealthy people. Their vast empire spread 3,100 miles (5,000 km) through the Andes mountain range of South America. They worshipped the Sun as a god.

The Inca built a network of roads across their mountain empire. Rope suspension bridges crossed deep ravines. Servants carried important people along the roads in litters.

THE AZTEC

The Aztec ruled a huge area of what is now Mexico. They conquered many local tribes. They had a huge army of trained soldiers. The fearsome jaguar warriors (right) were soldiers who had captured many enemies. The Aztecan capital, Tenochtitlán, was a magnificent city built in the middle of a lake. The city had many temples, each built in the shape of a step pyramid.

THE MAYA

The Maya of Central America played a tough game where players would try to get a ball through a hoop about 26 feet (8m) above the ground. They could only use their hips or elbows. The game was taken very seriously—the losers were put to death!

COLUMBUS

Christopher Columbus sailed from Spain across the Atlantic in 1492. He was looking for a route around the world. When he reached the islands of the Caribbean, he thought they were the East Indies. He claimed the land for Spain.

PIRATES

PIRATES are people who steal from ships. From the 16th to the 18th centuries, many pirates sailed across the oceans in stolen ships. They attacked other ships, took their cargo, and killed their crews. The Spanish Main (the southern Caribbean Sea) was very popular among pirates. In Europe, the Barbary Corsairs captured people to take back to North Africa to work as slaves.

Large ships, called galleons, were a favorite target for the smaller, faster pirate ships on the Spanish Main. The galleons often carried gold, jewelry, and coins ("pieces of eight").

The pirate flag was called the Jolly Roger.

INTO BATTLE!

Pirates often attacked a Spanish galleon by surprise. They raised the Jolly Roger only moments before they made their attack. After chasing the galleon, the pirate ship pulled up alongside. Then, armed with, razor-sharp, curved-edge swords, the pirates leaped aboard the ship. Some pirates also carried pistols and knives.

After a fierce battle with the ship's crew, the pirates threw the captain overboard. They then took all the treasure, weapons, and food they could find before sailing away.

CAPTAIN COOK

IN 1768 very little was known about the South Seas. People thought there must be a huge continent there. To discover more, the British sailor James Cook was sent on a great expedition around the world.

Cook's ship, *Endeavour*, was an old coal carrier. It was sturdy and slow-moving, but it had plenty of storage space for fresh food. It survived storms and even a shipwreck.

TO THE SOUTH SEAS

Cook sailed first to the Pacific island of Tahiti. Next he arrived in New Zealand and met the fierce Maori, seen here in their war canoes (above). Then he sailed west to Australia.

James Cook was born in Yorkshire, England, in 1728. He went to sea at the age of 18 and became one of the navy's best seamen.

Cook's men were astonished by the unusual animals they saw in Australia. Cook said that kangaroos were as big as sheep and jumped like hares. He also said they were very good to eat!

LIFE ON BOARD SHIP

It was very cramped on the *Endeavour*. The ceiling was so low below decks that the crew had to bend over as they walked. But Cook looked after his men well and brought the *Endeavour* safely back to England in 1772. He had sailed all around the world. Cook went on two more great voyages to the Pacific Ocean. In Hawaii the native people thought he was a god. But when Cook returned there in 1779, he argued with them over a stolen boat. There was a violent struggle, and Cook was killed.

THE PLAINS INDIANS

TWO hundred years ago, people roamed the Great Plains of North America. Some lived in tribes and hunted buffalo for food and skins. When the herds of buffalo moved on, the people followed them across the plains.

drying meat

learning archery

scraping hides

carrying a baby

LIVING IN A TEPEE

Every family lived in its own tepee—a tent made from buffalo skins stretched over a frame of poles. It could be put up and taken down again quickly and packed away when the tribe moved on. Inside the tepee was a fire for keeping warm and for cooking. Smoke escaped through a hole in the top. The men hunted buffalo on horseback with bows and arrows. Women dried or cooked the meat. They prepared the buffalo skins by scraping them and drying them in the sun.

travois (a carrier dragged by horses or people)

inside a tepee

THE GOLD RUSH

IN 1848 James Marshall discovered gold near Sacramento, California. By 1849 over 90,000 men, called "forty-niners" after the year, had flocked to the area hoping to make their fortune. Very few succeeded. Even if they found gold, it was usually too expensive to mine it.

entrance to gold mine

panning for gold

PANNING FOR GOLD

The miners looked for gold in the mud of river beds. Some built rough wooden channels, hoping to trap fragments of gold in them. Others simply scooped up mud into pans or wooden troughs. Water washed the lighter dirt away, leaving any gold dust behind.

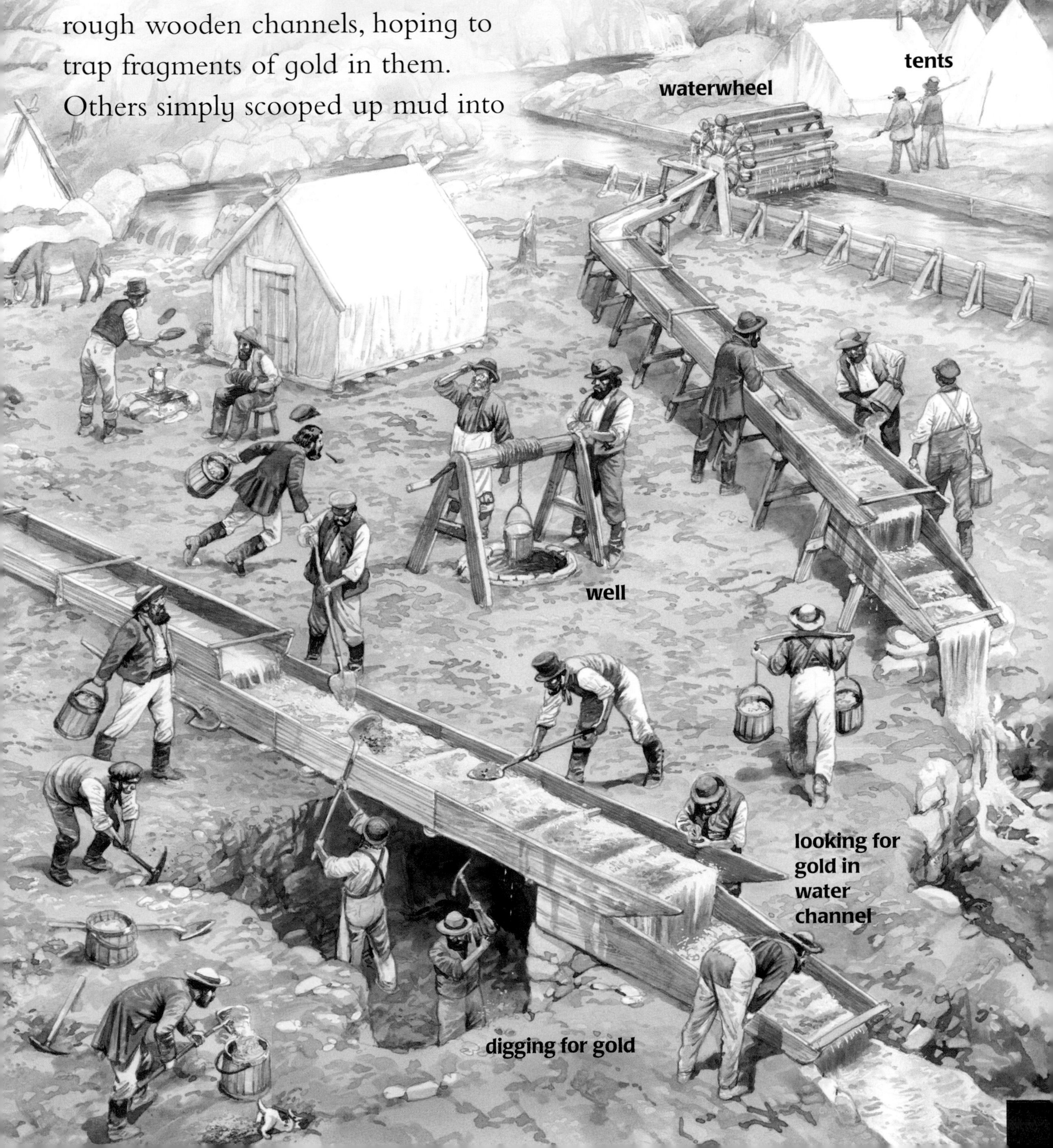

tents

waterwheel

well

looking for gold in water channel

digging for gold

A WILD WEST TOWN

BY THE 1870s, railways linked the Great Plains to the rich cities in the East. Cowboys herded their cattle across the plains to the railway towns. The cattle were taken by train to be sold at market.

stagecoach

saloon

cattle being driven into town

LIFE IN A CATTLE TOWN

Busy towns grew up on the plains close to the railways. The cattle were driven by cowboys along cattle trails from ranches in Texas. After their long journey, the cowboys were eager to take a bath, shave, and get their hair cut. They bought new clothes to replace their old ones, which were too dirty to keep. To have some fun, they went to saloons and dance halls.

cattle being herded onto a train

steam train

ELITE LODGINGS

LIVERY

stables

cowboys

A ZULU VILLAGE

THE ZULU people of southern Africa were farmers and warriors. Their cattle were very important to them, as they provided both food and clothing. In the 19th century, under King Shaka, the Zulu became a powerful nation.

stores

A ZULU HOMESTEAD

In this scene, a Zulu clan is preparing for a ceremony. The chief and his warriors are dressed to do a traditional war dance. It was the job of the men and boys to look after the cattle and defend the clan. The boys learned to be warriors, too. The chief had several wives and many children. Zulu women cared for the children, tended the crops, and collected water from rivers. They carried it in large pots balanced on their heads. The women made beautiful beadwork and prepared skins from the cattle to make clothes and shields.

warriors

preparing skins

A STREET 150 YEARS AGO

CITIES grew rapidly during the 19th century in Europe and North America. With the coming of industry, workers were needed for the new mills and factories. Railways were built to make it easier to transport people and goods. Many people moved from the countryside to the towns.

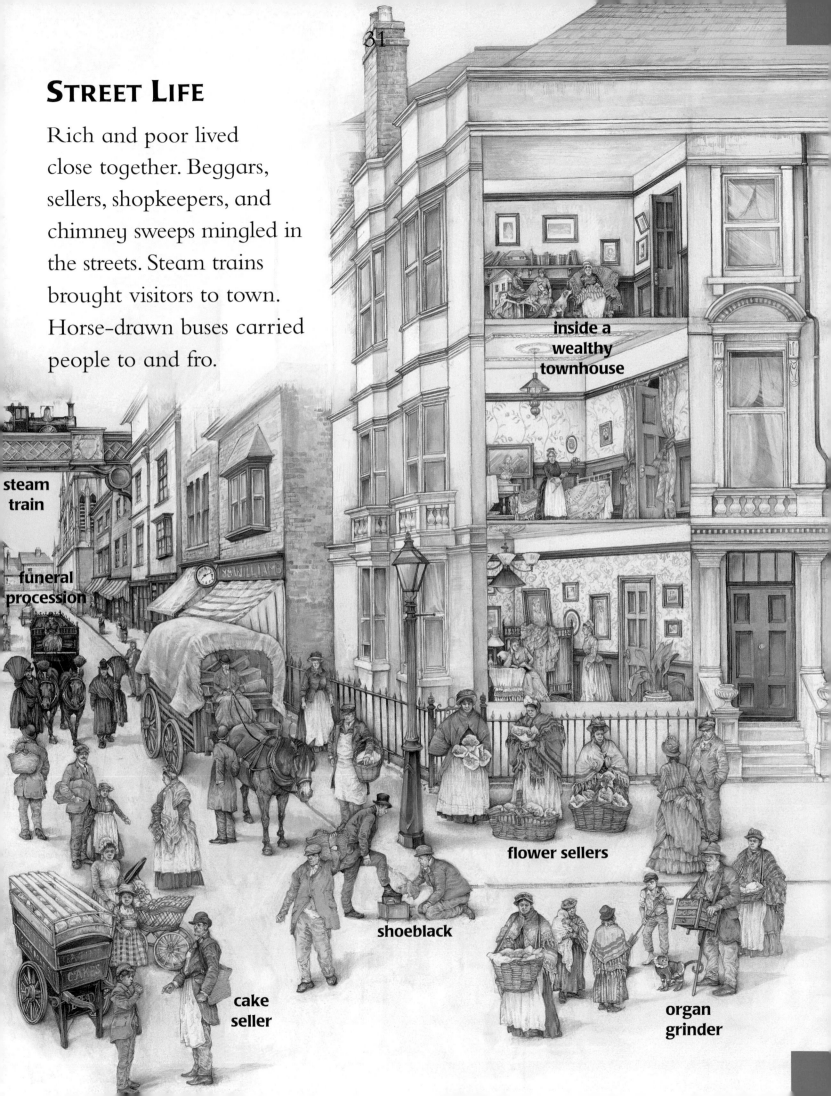

STREET LIFE

Rich and poor lived close together. Beggars, sellers, shopkeepers, and chimney sweeps mingled in the streets. Steam trains brought visitors to town. Horse-drawn buses carried people to and fro.

inside a wealthy townhouse

steam train

funeral procession

flower sellers

shoeblack

cake seller

organ grinder

GLOSSARY

dictator a ruler who has absolute power

jousting fighting, especially on horseback

litters covered chairs or couches with shafts, on which people are carried by other people

martial arts arts of combat and self-defense

pagodas towers, usually with roofs that curve upwards

thatched covered with a plant material such as straw

INDEX

A
Americas 16–17
armies 6–7, 12
Australia 20–21
Aztec 16–17

B
bailey 8–9
Barbary Corsairs, 18
battles 6–7, 19
blacksmiths 5, 8, 11, 27
boats 4, 13
buses 31

C
canoes 20
castles 7, 8–9, 11, 15
cathedral 11
cattle 26–27, 28–29
ceremonies 29
China 12–13
Christians 6
cities 10–11, 30–31
Columbus, Christopher 17
conquistadors 16
Constantinople 6
Cook, James 20–21
cowboys 26–27
craftspeople 4, 11
crusaders 6–7
Crusades 6–7

DEFG
dance 29
emperors 12–13

Endeavour 20–21
Europe 4–5, 6, 8–9, 10–11, 18, 30
explorers 4, 13, 17, 20–21
factories 30
farming 11, 12, 15, 28
"forty-niners" 24
galleons 18–19
gold 13, 24–25
gold rush 24–25

H
harbor 4
Hawaii 21
horsemen 7, 12, 15
hunting 12, 22–23

IJK
Inca 16
industry 30
Japan 14–15
Jerusalem 6–7
Jolly Roger 18–19
jousting 9
junks 13
kangaroos 21
keep 8–9
kings 8, 9, 28
knights 6–7, 9
Knights Templar 7
Kublai Khan 12–13

LMN
longboats 4

lords 8, 9
Maori 20
markets 4–5, 10–11, 26
Marshall, James 24
martial arts 15
Maya 16, 17
medieval castles 8–9
medieval China 12–13
medieval cities 10–11
medieval Japan 14–15
merchants 10–11
Middle Ages 10–11, 12–13
mills 30
Mongols 12
monks 7
Muslims 6–7
New Zealand 20
North America 4, 22–23, 24–25, 26–27, 30

P
palaces 12–13
pirates 18–19
Plains Indians, 22–23
Polo, Marco 13

RS
railways 26, 27, 30
roads, 16

Saint John's Hospitallers 7
Saladin 7
saloons 26–27
Samurai 14–15
Saracens 7
Shaka (Zulu king) 28
Shangdu 13
ships 18, 20, 21
shogun, 14
Silk Road 12
solar 8
stagecoaches 26

T
Tahiti 20
temples 17
Tenochtitlán 17
tepees 23
thatching 5, 11
tournaments 9
trade 11, 12
trains 26, 27, 31
travois 23

VWZ
Vikings 4–5
warriors 5, 14, 17, 28, 29
workshops 4
Zheng He 13
Zulu 28–29